Designed for Purpose

*You are designed for purpose!*

*Tonya Pinna*

Jan se couzend !
Jan se jouepte
Jean Paris

A Reflective Journal

# DESIGNED FOR PURPOSE

Discovering God's Daily Direction

# TANYA PRINCE

NASHVILLE

NEW YORK • LONDON • MELBOURNE • VANCOUVER

# Designed for Purpose

## Discovering God's Daily Direction

© 2025 Tanya Prince

All rights reserved. No portion of this book may be reproduced, stored in a retrieval system, or transmitted in any form or by any means—electronic, mechanical, photocopy, recording, scanning, or other—except for brief quotations in critical reviews or articles, without the prior written permission of the publisher.

Published in New York, New York, by Morgan James Publishing. Morgan James is a trademark of Morgan James, LLC. www.MorganJamesPublishing.com

Proudly distributed by Publishers Group West®

Scripture quotations taken from the (NASB®) New American Standard Bible®, Copyright © 1960, 1971, 1977, 1995, 2020 by The Lockman Foundation. Used by permission. All rights reserved. Lockman.org

Scripture quotations marked (NIV) are taken from the Holy Bible, New International Version®, NIV®. Copyright © 1973, 1978, 1984, 2011 by Biblica, Inc.™ Used by permission of Zondervan. All rights reserved worldwide. www.zondervan.com The "NIV" and "New International Version" are trademarks registered in the United States Patent and Trademark Office by Biblica, Inc.™

Scripture taken from the New King James Version®. Copyright © 1982 by Thomas Nelson. Used by permission. All rights reserved.

Scripture quotations marked (NLT) are taken from the *Holy Bible*, New Living Translation, copyright ©1996, 2004, 2015 by Tyndale House Foundation. Used by permission of Tyndale House Publishers, Carol Stream, Illinois 60188. All rights reserved.

Scripture taken from the Holy Scriptures, Tree of Life Version*. Copyright © 2014, 2016 by the Tree of Life Bible Society. Used by permission of the Tree of Life Bible Society

**A FREE** ebook edition is available for you or a friend with the purchase of this print book.

CLEARLY SIGN YOUR NAME ABOVE

**Instructions to claim your free ebook edition:**
1. Visit MorganJamesBOGO.com
2. Sign your name CLEARLY in the space above
3. Complete the form and submit a photo of this entire page
4. You or your friend can download the ebook to your preferred device

ISBN 9781636985138 paperback
ISBN 9781636985145 ebook
Library of Congress Control Number: 2024941223

**Cover & Interior Design by:**
Christopher Kirk
www.GFSstudio.com

Morgan James is a proud partner of Habitat for Humanity Peninsula and Greater Williamsburg. Partners in building since 2006.

Get involved today! Visit: www.morgan-james-publishing.com/giving-back

# CONTENTS

Introduction . . . . . . . . . . . . . . . . . . . . . . . . . . . . . . . . . . . . . . . . . 1
Four-Week Journey . . . . . . . . . . . . . . . . . . . . . . . . . . . . . . . . . . . 3
Daily Reflection. . . . . . . . . . . . . . . . . . . . . . . . . . . . . . . . . . . . . . 5

Week One: Designed for Purpose . . . . . . . . . . . . . . . . . . . . . . . . 8
Week Two: Submitting Your Purpose. . . . . . . . . . . . . . . . . . . . .38
Week Three: Discerning Your Purpose . . . . . . . . . . . . . . . . . . . .68
Week Four: Choosing Your Purpose. . . . . . . . . . . . . . . . . . . . . .98
Close: Stepping Into Your Purpose. . . . . . . . . . . . . . . . . . . . . .128

Your Purpose Journey Is Just Beginning. . . . . . . . . . . . . . . . . . .133
About the Author . . . . . . . . . . . . . . . . . . . . . . . . . . . . . . . . . .141

# INTRODUCTION

*For we are God's handiwork, created in Christ Jesus to do good works, which God prepared in advance for us to do.*
*Ephesians 2:10 (NIV)*

"I just want to know what God wants me to do!" Is this a common question you hear yourself saying to your friends, to yourself, and in your prayer life? God promises us in Matthew 7:7–8, "Ask and it will be given to you; seek and you will find; knock and the door will be opened to you. For everyone who asks receives; the one who seeks finds; and to the one who knocks, the door will be opened" (NIV). Why does it sometimes seem that there is no answer? We all go through seasons in which it seems the Lord is silent, but too often today, it may be that we simply aren't taking the time to listen. Are our lives so busy and noisy that we can't hear His "still small voice" (1 Kings 19:12 NKJV), let alone a megaphone?

Scripture repeatedly tells us that we are meant to have a good and wonderful purpose in our lives. The prophet Jeremiah wrote, "'For I know the plans I have for you,' declares the Lord, 'plans to prosper you and not to harm you, plans to give you hope and a future. Then you will call on me and come and pray to me, and I will listen to you. You will seek me and find me when you seek me with all your heart'" (Jeremiah 29:11–13 NIV). The first part of this verse, Jeremiah 29:11, is often quoted, and with good reason! It is true; God does have a good plan for you. In fact, it is an amazing plan, intended for you to thrive and prosper as you live in constant hope for the future. However, it is incomplete without the second part, Jeremiah 29:12, in which we, because of this promise, draw close and call to Him and pray to Him. God's plans for us don't just passively happen. His plans are part of our relationship *with Him*. We are called to seek Him in this plan, and He promises to listen and to be found. The God of the universe is saying He will listen and respond to us when we seek Him out! Are you actively seeking Him, or are you passively waiting for revelation? If you are ready to know God's great purpose and plan for your life, then it's time to ask, seek, knock, call, and pray.

# FOUR-WEEK JOURNEY

This four-week journal is meant to help you both pursue the Lord for His purpose and direction and to hear and see His response in your life each day.

During this four-week journey, you will reflect daily on six areas:

- Experiences that create joy, happiness, and fulfillment in your spirit
- Experiences that generate concern and response in your spirit
- People, events, and things for which you are grateful
- Encounters of doubts, fears, obstacles, and setbacks
- The truth of your identity and strength in Christ
- Evidence of God's intervention, sovereignty, confirmation, and voice

These six topics are designed to cultivate a heart of reflection, perception, and discernment.

Each week is organized with a theme, a verse, and an exercise to prepare you for the week ahead and focus your observations and reflections. The weekly exercise helps you to take prayerful action steps toward your purpose.

Each day includes a verse aligned with one of the six areas of reflection and is a starting point to prepare your heart and mind for discernment and connection with the Lord. The verses are a glimpse of how scripture carries the voice of God in directing you and of His character in walking with you. Each day also includes a time for prayer and overall reflection for you to seek Him and respond to Him as you grow in your understanding of His will for your life.

At the end of the week, you will reflect on the past days to observe and consider the reoccurrence of situations, events, ideas, and feelings. Often the Lord confirms His guidance through the convergence of inspiration, words spoken through people, unexpected events, and scripture. You may begin to see doors that clearly open or close and a sense of pulling toward and away from places, people, and tasks. Sunday's verses help you understand the Lord's will for taking action and making decisions. After careful contemplation and discernment, bring your thoughts before the Lord in prayer, asking Him to confirm your sincere desire to follow His leading and direction.

# DAILY REFLECTION

The six categories of reflection are a guide to help you carefully examine how you interact with the world around you and discern your purpose in it. In reflection, you will seek evidence of your purpose by considering how you emotionally, physically, mentally, and spiritually responded to the events of the day. The daily verses are aligned with one of the six categories and provide a scriptural foundation for the reflections.

## I found joy, happiness, and fulfillment in …

The Lord gave us good desires and passions. When we live in our purpose, the Bible tells us that we produce "good fruit" (Matthew 7:17 NIV) in many forms. When our talents and passion come together in the space of purpose, we can feel a sense of accomplishment, meaning, and fulfillment. Our work produces a beneficial impact, our character in performing the effort demonstrates positive attributes, and our outcomes may multiply. Feelings of joy and excitement may flow through you and overflow to those around you. When your talents are aligned with your purpose, you will discover that they can be applied in new and exciting ways, and it gives you new motivation and creativity. This reflection may include gratifying steps toward a goal or dream you've had for some time, or it may include the discovery of a new path for the first time. Monday's scriptures describe the affirming nature of experiencing purpose in our work.

## I felt concern and response to …

Scripture tells us that "Each of you should use whatever gift you have received to serve others" (1 Peter 4:10 NIV). Because of our purpose, we are uniquely crafted to feel a pull to solve particular problems or engage in meeting certain needs when we see them. You may experience an overwhelming sense of empathy, grief, or anger in response to an issue, injustice, or hardship in the world or in the lives of those around you. Tuesday's verses illustrate the nature of how we can be called to use our gifts to serve others and the heart of God for His people.

## I felt gratitude for ...

God reminds us that "every good and perfect gift is from above" (James 1:17 NIV). Gratitude helps us to observe God's intervention and provision in our lives. It helps us look beyond the surface to notice how past challenges or circumstances have woven together over time to form a beneficial outcome. It takes our eyes off our current concerns and reminds us that God has provided and will continue to provide. As you examine your day with thankfulness, consider how the people and things you are grateful for came to be. Perhaps a close friend was brought into your life at just the right time, or a job loss turned into an unexpected opportunity. Wednesday's scriptures demonstrate the nature of God's care for you and participation in your life now and in the future.

## I experienced doubt, fear, obstacles, or setbacks in ...

Our lives are not free from pain, turmoil, loss, and setbacks in our journey to discovering and living out our God-given purpose. When we begin to experience our true identity in Christ, we may feel sudden and unexplainable doubt, fear, negative thoughts, or even discouragement and hurt from people around us.

Scripture gives us many reasons why we may encounter difficult and challenging circumstances. Jesus warned that "the thief comes only to steal and kill and destroy" (John 10:10 NIV). Recognizing and releasing fears and hurts is a crucial step to advancing in your purpose. Obstacles and setbacks can also occur because of our own choices. Sometimes we choose to go where God has told us not to go or give in to a temptation that leads to negative consequences. We may try to fill a need because we have the skill, but we don't have the passion or calling. The Bible also tells us that God does allow testing and obstacles in our life so that we will grow and be prepared to take on the next phase of our life's purpose. Finally, sometimes we experience failure or a painful experience outside our control, and there simply is no explanation for why God has allowed it to happen. God wants us to bring all these things to Him.

In this reflection, release the challenging experiences of the day. Assess the circumstances, evaluate your actions and choices, and carefully consider what you can learn from the situation. Thursday's verses illustrate the ways in which God desires to guide you through fear, doubt, obstacles, and setbacks.

## I remember my identity and strength because ...

God tells us that we are His "workmanship" (Ephesians 2:10 NKJV) and that "before I formed you in the womb I knew you, before you were born I set you apart" (Jeremiah 1:5 NIV). He wants us to constantly remember how valuable we are to Him and to be secure in who He designed us to be. Your unique combination of skills and abilities, your personality, and your unique characteristics are by God's specific design.

In addition to designing us for purpose, God tells us, "Have I not commanded you? Be strong and courageous. Do not be afraid; do not be discouraged, for the Lord your God will be with you wherever you go" (Joshua 1:9 NIV). God does not want us to be timid in pursuing His dreams and purpose for us. He wants us to be strengthened and encouraged by the truth of His word, our trustworthy friends, and His physical and spiritual presence.

In this reflection, think about the wonderful qualities God has equipped you with and the many promises He has made to you in His word. Friday's scriptures communicate how God sees you, loves you, values you, and strengthens you.

## I saw God move today in ...

God is a real and living God who is tangible and observable. He directs us, "Ask and it will be given to you; seek and you will find" (Matthew 7:7 NIV). He is telling us to actively engage Him and to expect a response! God responds to us in many different forms. He speaks through scripture that connects with your heart and mind. He uses friends who reach out to you or provide you with prayerful advice when you share your concerns and questions with them. He gives you the right song at the right moment. He imparts hopes and dreams in you while you are awake and asleep. He may speak audibly in your ear, shout a repeating thought in your mind, or whisper deeply to your spirit. God also brings together unexplainable connections and experiences in your day or over time in your life that make His intervention visible and clear to you. Saturday's verses illustrate God's voice and His tangible actions to guide those who desire to be led by Him.

# WEEK ONE
# DESIGNED FOR PURPOSE

*And we know that God causes all things to work together for good to those who love God, to those who are called according to His purpose.*
**Romans 8:28 (NASB)**

You were created uniquely and perfectly to fill a role in this world. No one can replace the contributions you have to give to your family, your community, and the world. Each day, your purpose is being woven together and the God of the universe, your Good Father, is calling you to it. He is moving the pieces of your life and desires you to see it.

## Exercise

Make a list of your skills, talents, and capabilities. Are you very good at a particular skill? What comes easily and naturally to you? What are your strengths? Is there something that you are very effective or efficient at doing? What do you enjoy doing? What characteristics do you bring to a task that others appreciate in you? You may wish to ask a friend or family member about their observations for additional perspective or take an online assessment. Place the list in front of you and pray to the Lord. Thank Him for the wonderful way He has designed you. Pray that He will reveal to you the talents and abilities He has given you and ask Him to show you how He wants you to use these gifts in the week ahead.

## The week ahead

This week, begin to take notice of all the ways in which He has designed you and how He is guiding you. It could be through a conversation with a friend, through a spark that filled you with energy, or a nudge to action. Each evening, find a quiet place to reflect on your day. Consider the events of the day, the emotions you felt, and the thoughts that came into your mind. Consider whether using your talents and skills in an activity brought you joy or irritation. Evaluate where you felt your mind, body, and spirit aligned in a task and where you felt you were compromising or moving in the wrong direction. Spend time in prayer asking God to help you see Him and hear Him throughout the week.

Notes

## 10 | DESIGNED FOR PURPOSE

Date: _____

Week 1, Day 1

### I found joy, happiness, and fulfillment in ...

_____
_____
_____
_____
_____

### I felt concern and response to ...

_____
_____
_____
_____
_____

### I felt gratitude for ...

_____
_____
_____
_____
_____

*A cheerful heart is good medicine, but a
crushed spirit dries up the bones.*
**Proverbs 17:22 (NIV)**

I experienced doubt, fear, obstacles, or setbacks in ...

_____

_____

_____

_____

I remember my identity and strength because ...

_____

_____

_____

_____

I saw God move today in ...

_____

_____

_____

_____

## Journaling and Prayer

Journaling and Prayer

# 14 | DESIGNED FOR PURPOSE

Date: _____

Week 1, Day 2

### I found joy, happiness, and fulfillment in ...

_____

_____

_____

_____

### I felt concern and response to ...

_____

_____

_____

_____

_____

### I felt gratitude for ...

_____

_____

_____

_____

_____

# WEEK 1, DAY 2 | 15

*As he approached Jerusalem and
saw the city, he wept over it.*
**Luke 19:41 (NIV)**

I experienced doubt, fear, obstacles, or setbacks in …

_____
_____
_____
_____

I remember my identity and strength because …

_____
_____
_____
_____

I saw God move today in …

_____
_____
_____
_____

## Journaling and Prayer

## Journaling and Prayer

# 18 | DESIGNED FOR PURPOSE

Date: _____

Week 1, Day 3

I found joy, happiness, and fulfillment in …

_____
_____
_____
_____
_____

I felt concern and response to …

_____
_____
_____
_____
_____

I felt gratitude for …

_____
_____
_____
_____
_____

*Every good and perfect gift is from above,
coming down from the Father of the heavenly lights,
who does not change like shifting shadows.*
**James 1:17 (NIV)**

I experienced doubt, fear, obstacles, or setbacks in ...

_____
_____
_____
_____
_____

I remember my identity and strength because ...

_____
_____
_____
_____
_____

I saw God move today in ...

_____
_____
_____
_____
_____

## Journaling and Prayer

Journaling and Prayer

## DESIGNED FOR PURPOSE

Date: _____
Week 1, Day 4

### I found joy, happiness, and fulfillment in ...

_____
_____
_____
_____
_____

### I felt concern and response to ...

_____
_____
_____
_____
_____

### I felt gratitude for ...

_____
_____
_____
_____
_____

# WEEK 1, DAY 4 | 23

*Stay alert! Watch out for your great enemy, the devil.
He prowls around like a roaring lion, looking for someone
to devour. Stand firm against him, and be strong in your faith.*
**1 Peter 5:8–9 (NLT)**

I experienced doubt, fear, obstacles, or setbacks in ...

_____
_____
_____
_____

I remember my identity and strength because ...

_____
_____
_____
_____

I saw God move today in ...

_____
_____
_____
_____

## 24 | DESIGNED FOR PURPOSE

### Journaling and Prayer

WEEK 1, DAY 4 | 25

Journaling and Prayer

# DESIGNED FOR PURPOSE

Date: _____

Week 1, Day 5

### I found joy, happiness, and fulfillment in ...

_____

_____

_____

_____

### I felt concern and response to ...

_____

_____

_____

_____

### I felt gratitude for ...

_____

_____

_____

_____

# WEEK 1, DAY 5 | 27

*Thank you for making me so wonderfully complex!*
*Your workmanship is marvelous—how well I know it.*
**Psalms 139:14 (NLT)**

I experienced doubt, fear, obstacles, or setbacks in ...

_____
_____
_____
_____

I remember my identity and strength because ...

_____
_____
_____
_____

I saw God move today in ...

_____
_____
_____
_____

# DESIGNED FOR PURPOSE

## Journaling and Prayer

## Journaling and Prayer

30 | DESIGNED FOR PURPOSE

Date: _____

Week 1, Day 6

I found joy, happiness, and fulfillment in ...

_____
_____
_____
_____

I felt concern and response to ...

_____
_____
_____
_____

I felt gratitude for ...

_____
_____
_____
_____

# WEEK 1, DAY 6 | 31

*Then you will call on me and come and pray to me,
and I will listen to you. You will seek me and find me
when you seek me with all your heart.*
*Jeremiah 29:12–13 (NIV)*

I experienced doubt, fear, obstacles, or setbacks in ...

_____

_____

_____

_____

I remember my identity and strength because ...

_____

_____

_____

_____

I saw God move today in ...

_____

_____

_____

_____

## Journaling and Prayer

# WEEK 1, DAY 6 | 33

Journaling and Prayer

Date: _____
Week 1, Day 7

Reoccurring events, emotions, thoughts, words ...

_____
_____
_____
_____
_____

I felt encouraged and strengthened by (people, events, situations) ...

_____
_____
_____
_____
_____

I encouraged others by ...

_____
_____
_____
_____
_____

*Sow your seed in the morning, and at evening let your
hands not be idle, for you do not know which will succeed,
whether this or that, or whether both will do equally well.*
*Ecclesiastes 11:6 (NIV)*

I am sensing a direction toward or away from ...

_____

_____

_____

_____

Next week I will be intentional to ...

_____

_____

_____

_____

Prayer for guidance and direction in ...

_____

_____

_____

_____

## Journaling and Prayer

# WEEK 1, DAY 7 | 37

## Journaling and Prayer

# WEEK TWO
# SUBMITTING YOUR PURPOSE

*I will instruct you and teach you in the way you should go;
I will counsel you with my loving eye on you.*
**Psalm 32:8 (NIV)**

God promises to instruct and teach you in His purpose for you. He is not a God who keeps Himself from you or is distant. Throughout your day, He is counseling you on the direction to take, building your senses to recognize the good desires He has given you, and making you sensitive to the world around you. He is teaching you to discern as you seek Him, and when you make a mistake, He lovingly guides you back to His path for you.

## Exercise

Make a list of the significant choices you have made in your life. What choices have led to positive outcomes for you and what choices have led to difficult consequences? Evaluate the underlying factors that led you to make each choice. What desire were you seeking to fulfill? Who influenced your thinking and emotions in the decision? Did you see signals along the way that you ignored or acted upon? Place this list in front of you. Pray to the Lord, thanking Him for the good outcomes in your life and for the people who care about you and help you make good decisions. Ask Him for forgiveness and healing for your choices that have led to difficulties and pain. Accept His fresh start for you, tell Him that you want His counsel in your life, and ask Him for the strength to follow His direction.

## The week ahead

This week, evaluate the small and large choices you are making each day as you work through your reflections. Pray to the Lord each morning and before each decision, asking Him to align your decision-making with His purpose for you. As you observe the real-time outcomes of current and prior choices, consider what signals, feelings, or nudges you noticed before, during, and after the decision. In prayer, express your gratitude for His leading or ask for forgiveness as you seek His gentle correction. Each evening, find a quiet place to reflect on your day and the choices you made, considering the mental, physical, and emotional factors that contributed to your decision-making. Prayerfully ask the Lord for His blessing and guidance as you bring your decisions to Him.

## Notes

Date: _____

Week 2, Day 1

### I found joy, happiness, and fulfillment in ...

_____
_____
_____
_____
_____

### I felt concern and response to ...

_____
_____
_____
_____
_____

### I felt gratitude for ...

_____
_____
_____
_____
_____

*Take delight in the LORD, and he
will give you the desires of your heart.*
**Psalm 37:4 (NIV)**

I experienced doubt, fear, obstacles, or setbacks in ...

_____

_____

_____

_____

I remember my identity and strength because ...

_____

_____

_____

_____

I saw God move today in ...

_____

_____

_____

_____

## Journaling and Prayer

## Journaling and Prayer

Date: _____

Week 2, Day 2

I found joy, happiness, and fulfillment in ...

_____
_____
_____
_____
_____

I felt concern and response to ...

_____
_____
_____
_____
_____

I felt gratitude for ...

_____
_____
_____
_____
_____

*Do not be overcome by evil,
but overcome evil with good.*
**Romans 12:21 (NIV)**

I experienced doubt, fear, obstacles, or setbacks in …

_____

_____

_____

_____

I remember my identity and strength because …

_____

_____

_____

_____

I saw God move today in …

_____

_____

_____

_____

## Journaling and Prayer

Journaling and Prayer

Date: _____

Week 2, Day 3

I found joy, happiness, and fulfillment in ...

_____
_____
_____
_____

I felt concern and response to ...

_____
_____
_____
_____

I felt gratitude for ...

_____
_____
_____
_____

# WEEK 2, DAY 3 | 49

*Give thanks in all circumstances;*
*for this is God's will for you in Christ Jesus.*
***1 Thessalonians 5:18 (NIV)***

I experienced doubt, fear, obstacles, or setbacks in ...

___

___

___

___

I remember my identity and strength because ...

___

___

___

___

I saw God move today in ...

___

___

___

___

## Journaling and Prayer

# WEEK 2, DAY 3

## Journaling and Prayer

## 52 | DESIGNED FOR PURPOSE

Date: _____
Week 2, Day 4

I found joy, happiness, and fulfillment in ...

_____
_____
_____
_____
_____

I felt concern and response to ...

_____
_____
_____
_____
_____

I felt gratitude for ...

_____
_____
_____
_____
_____

*As far as the east is from the west, so far has he removed our transgressions from us. As a father has compassion on his children, so the LORD has compassion on those who fear him.*
**Psalm 103:12-13 (NIV)**

I experienced doubt, fear, obstacles, or setbacks in …

_____
_____
_____
_____

I remember my identity and strength because …

_____
_____
_____
_____

I saw God move today in …

_____
_____
_____
_____

## Journaling and Prayer

## Journaling and Prayer

Date: _____

Week 2, Day 5

I found joy, happiness, and fulfillment in ...

_____
_____
_____
_____

I felt concern and response to ...

_____
_____
_____
_____

I felt gratitude for ...

_____
_____
_____
_____

*For God has not given us a spirit of fear and timidity,
but of power, love, and self-discipline.*
**2 Timothy 1:7 (NLT)**

I experienced doubt, fear, obstacles, or setbacks in ...

_____
_____
_____
_____

I remember my identity and strength because ...

_____
_____
_____
_____

I saw God move today in ...

_____
_____
_____
_____

## Journaling and Prayer

## Journaling and Prayer

Date: _____

Week 2, Day 6

### I found joy, happiness, and fulfillment in ...

_____

_____

_____

_____

### I felt concern and response to ...

_____

_____

_____

_____

_____

### I felt gratitude for ...

_____

_____

_____

_____

_____

# WEEK 2, DAY 6 | 61

*"Ask and it will be given to you; seek and you will find; knock and the door will be opened to you. For everyone who asks receives; the one who seeks finds; and to the one who knocks, the door will be opened."*
*Matthew 7:7–8 (NIV)*

I experienced doubt, fear, obstacles, or setbacks in ...

_____

_____

_____

_____

_____

I remember my identity and strength because ...

_____

_____

_____

_____

_____

I saw God move today in ...

_____

_____

_____

_____

_____

## Journaling and Prayer

## Journaling and Prayer

# 64 | DESIGNED FOR PURPOSE

Date: _____
Week 2, Day 7

Reoccurring events, emotions, thoughts, words ...

_____
_____
_____
_____
_____

I felt encouraged and strengthened by (people, events, situations) ...

_____
_____
_____
_____
_____

I encouraged others by ...

_____
_____
_____
_____
_____

*Enthusiasm without knowledge is no good; haste makes mistakes. People ruin their lives by their own foolishness and then are angry at the LORD.*
**Proverbs 19:2–3 (NLT)**

I am sensing a direction toward or away from ...

Next week I will be intentional to ...

Prayer for guidance and direction in ...

## Journaling and Prayer

# Journaling and Prayer

# WEEK THREE
# DISCERNING YOUR PURPOSE

*"For I know the plans I have for you," declares the LORD,*
*"plans to prosper you and not to harm you,*
*plans to give you hope and a future."*
*Jeremiah 29:11 (NIV)*

The Lord has a wonderful plan for your life. His design of you was precise and not in error in any way. He placed hopes and dreams in your heart, and you experience His purpose for you when you feel ignited and passionate in your pursuits. When you are outside of His purpose and plans, you may feel frustration, a lack of energy, or a sense of going through the motions. These feelings can help guide you, but feelings without discernment can also lead you in the wrong direction. In fact, scripture tells us that we can expect challenges and barriers, along with periods of frustration and uncertainty. Scripture even describes how some difficulties are specifically meant to help you grow and be refined so that you can go even further in your dreams. The key is learning to bring all your plans, feelings, opportunities, and barriers to the Lord in prayer, earnestly seeking to align your plans with His plans, then slowing down to observe what happens next.

## Exercise

Review your calendar for the week ahead. Evaluate each item and ask yourself, "Am I excited about this task or am I dreading it?" Does your energy increase or decrease when you consider the planned item? Do you feel a sense of excitement to use your gifts and skills, or do you feel you are doing it because you "have to"? Do you feel your calendar is missing something important to you? How many items are aligned with the dreams you have for your life? Place your schedule in front of you. Pray to the Lord, asking Him to show you where your plans are His plans and where your plans are not His plans.

## The week ahead

Each day, consider how the activities on your calendar are impacting your mind, body, and spirit as you work through your reflections. Did you sense a change in yourself before, during, or after the task or event? Did it bring out the best in you or the worst? In prayer, ask Him what He wants you to learn from your experiences and ask Him to reveal which priorities are aligned with His plans for you and which are not.

Notes

## DESIGNED FOR PURPOSE

Date: _____

Week 3, Day 1

### I found joy, happiness, and fulfillment in ...

_____
_____
_____
_____

### I felt concern and response to ...

_____
_____
_____
_____

### I felt gratitude for ...

_____
_____
_____
_____

## WEEK 3, DAY 1 | 71

*But the Holy Spirit produces this kind of fruit
in our lives: love, joy, peace, patience, kindness,
goodness, faithfulness, gentleness, and self-control.*
***Galatians 5:22-23 (NLT))***

I experienced doubt, fear, obstacles, or setbacks in ...

_____

_____

_____

_____

I remember my identity and strength because ...

_____

_____

_____

_____

I saw God move today in ...

_____

_____

_____

_____

## Journaling and Prayer

## Journaling and Prayer

Date: _____

Week 3, Day 2

I found joy, happiness, and fulfillment in ...

_____
_____
_____
_____

I felt concern and response to ...

_____
_____
_____
_____

I felt gratitude for ...

_____
_____
_____
_____

# WEEK 3, DAY 2 | 75

*As each one has received a gift, use it to serve one another, as good stewards of the many-sided grace of God.*
**1 Peter 4:10 (TLV)**

I experienced doubt, fear, obstacles, or setbacks in ...

_____
_____
_____
_____

I remember my identity and strength because ...

_____
_____
_____
_____

I saw God move today in ...

_____
_____
_____
_____

## Journaling and Prayer

## Journaling and Prayer

Date: _____

Week 3, Day 3

I found joy, happiness, and fulfillment in ...

_____
_____
_____
_____

I felt concern and response to ...

_____
_____
_____
_____

I felt gratitude for ...

_____
_____
_____
_____

*The LORD is my strength and shield. I trust him with
all my heart. He helps me, and my heart is filled
with joy. I burst out in songs of thanksgiving.*
**Psalm 28:7 (NLT)**

I experienced doubt, fear, obstacles, or setbacks in ...

I remember my identity and strength because ...

I saw God move today in ...

## Journaling and Prayer

## Journaling and Prayer

## 82 | DESIGNED FOR PURPOSE

Date: _____
Week 3, Day 4

I found joy, happiness, and fulfillment in ...

_____
_____
_____
_____

I felt concern and response to ...

_____
_____
_____
_____

I felt gratitude for ...

_____
_____
_____
_____

*When you pass through the waters, I will be with you; And through the rivers, they shall not overflow you. When you walk through the fire, you shall not be burned, Nor shall the flame scorch you.*
*Isaiah 43:2 (NKJV)*

I experienced doubt, fear, obstacles, or setbacks in ...

_____
_____
_____
_____
_____

I remember my identity and strength because ...

_____
_____
_____
_____
_____

I saw God move today in ...

_____
_____
_____
_____
_____

84 | DESIGNED FOR PURPOSE

## Journaling and Prayer

Journaling and Prayer

Date: _____

Week 3, Day 5

I found joy, happiness, and fulfillment in ...

_____
_____
_____
_____

I felt concern and response to ...

_____
_____
_____
_____

I felt gratitude for ...

_____
_____
_____
_____

# WEEK 3, DAY 5 | 87

*But you are a chosen generation, a royal priesthood, a holy nation,
His own special people, that you may proclaim the praises of Him
who called you out of darkness into His marvelous light.*
**1 Peter 2:9 (NKJV)**

I experienced doubt, fear, obstacles, or setbacks in ...

_____
_____
_____
_____
_____

I remember my identity and strength because ...

_____
_____
_____
_____
_____

I saw God move today in ...

_____
_____
_____
_____
_____

## Journaling and Prayer

## Journaling and Prayer

Date: _____

Week 3, Day 6

### I found joy, happiness, and fulfillment in ...

_____
_____
_____
_____
_____

### I felt concern and response to ...

_____
_____
_____
_____
_____

### I felt gratitude for ...

_____
_____
_____
_____
_____

> *But as for you, you meant evil against me; but God meant it for good, in order to bring it about as it is this day, to save many people alive.*
> **Genesis 50:20 (NKJV)**

I experienced doubt, fear, obstacles, or setbacks in ...

_____

_____

_____

_____

I remember my identity and strength because ...

_____

_____

_____

_____

I saw God move today in ...

_____

_____

_____

_____

## Journaling and Prayer

## Journaling and Prayer

94 | DESIGNED FOR PURPOSE

Date: _____
Week 3, Day 7

Reoccurring events, emotions, thoughts, words ...

_____
_____
_____
_____

I felt encouraged and strengthened by (people, events, situations) ...

_____
_____
_____
_____
_____

I encouraged others by ...

_____
_____
_____
_____

*Keep this Book of the Law always on your lips; meditate on it day and night, so that you may be careful to do everything written in it. Then you will be prosperous and successful.*
***Joshua 1:8 (NIV)***

I am sensing a direction toward or away from ...

_____

_____

_____

_____

Next week I will be intentional to ...

_____

_____

_____

_____

Prayer for guidance and direction in ...

_____

_____

_____

_____

## Journaling and Prayer

## Journaling and Prayer

# WEEK FOUR
# CHOOSING YOUR PURPOSE

> *"See, I am doing a new thing! Now it springs up;*
> *do you not perceive it? I am making a way*
> *in the wilderness and streams in the wasteland."*
> Isaiah 43:19 (NIV)

As you enter this final week of seeking, observing, and listening, take extra time in quietness. Seek to perceive how God is doing a new thing in you. He has stirred your heart, and as you grow, your eyes are seeing new things and your ears are hearing new whispers.

## Exercise

Make a list of your current commitments and priorities. This may include your family, career, volunteer work, or hobbies. Honestly consider where your time is going and what you prioritize first, second, third, and all the way to last.

Now make a second list of your dreams and goals for the future. What do you hope to create, accomplish, or impact in your life? Where do you want your time to be spent in the future? "Future" can be defined as one month from now, a year from now, or twenty years from now.

Place these two lists before you and pray over them, asking the Lord to help you specifically see His will for you in these things over the week ahead. Ask Him to help you perceive what He wants to change in your current and future plans.

## The week ahead

Each day this week, take out your lists during your journal and reflection time. Consider how the verses and reflection areas may apply. Where is the Lord prompting you to reduce or stop? Where do you need to exercise patience as you wait for the right timing? Where is He prompting you to expand or take action? Where has an opportunity opened? Where has a door closed? What new insights or inspiration do you have about your current priorities or your future dreams? What do you need to let go of and what do you need to embrace?

Notes

Date: _____

Week 4, Day 1

I found joy, happiness, and fulfillment in ...

I felt concern and response to ...

I felt gratitude for ...

*"The master was full of praise. 'Well done, my good and faithful servant. You have been faithful in handling this small amount, so now I will give you many more responsibilities. Let's celebrate together!'"*
*Matthew 25:21 (NLT)*

I experienced doubt, fear, obstacles, or setbacks in ...

_____

_____

_____

_____

I remember my identity and strength because ...

_____

_____

_____

_____

I saw God move today in ...

_____

_____

_____

_____

## Journaling and Prayer

## Journaling and Prayer

Date: _____
Week 4, Day 2

I found joy, happiness, and fulfillment in ...

_____
_____
_____
_____
_____

I felt concern and response to ...

_____
_____
_____
_____
_____

I felt gratitude for ...

_____
_____
_____
_____
_____

*Do not withhold good from those to whom
it is due, when it is in your power to act.*
**Proverbs 3:27 (NIV)**

I experienced doubt, fear, obstacles, or setbacks in ...

_____

_____

_____

_____

I remember my identity and strength because ...

_____

_____

_____

_____

I saw God move today in ...

_____

_____

_____

_____

## Journaling and Prayer

## Journaling and Prayer

Date: _____

Week 4, Day 3

I found joy, happiness, and fulfillment in ...

_____
_____
_____
_____

I felt concern and response to ...

_____
_____
_____
_____

I felt gratitude for ...

_____
_____
_____
_____

*But be sure to fear the LORD and serve him faithfully with all your heart; consider what great things he has done for you.*
**1 Samuel 12:24 (NIV)**

I experienced doubt, fear, obstacles, or setbacks in ...

_____

_____

_____

_____

I remember my identity and strength because ...

_____

_____

_____

_____

I saw God move today in ...

_____

_____

_____

_____

## Journaling and Prayer

## Journaling and Prayer

## DESIGNED FOR PURPOSE

Date: _____
Week 4, Day 4

I found joy, happiness, and fulfillment in ...

_____
_____
_____
_____

I felt concern and response to ...

_____
_____
_____
_____

I felt gratitude for ...

_____
_____
_____
_____

*Be very careful, then, how you live—not as unwise but as wise, making the most of every opportunity, because the days are evil.*
**Ephesians 5:15-16 (NIV)**

I experienced doubt, fear, obstacles, or setbacks in ...

_____

_____

_____

_____

I remember my identity and strength because ...

_____

_____

_____

_____

I saw God move today in ...

_____

_____

_____

_____

## Journaling and Prayer

Journaling and Prayer

Date: _____

Week 4, Day 5

### I found joy, happiness, and fulfillment in ...

_____
_____
_____
_____
_____

### I felt concern and response to ...

_____
_____
_____
_____
_____

### I felt gratitude for ...

_____
_____
_____
_____
_____

*So be strong and courageous! Do not be afraid and do not panic before them. For the LORD your God will personally go ahead of you. He will neither fail you nor abandon you.*
**Deuteronomy 31:6 (NLT)**

I experienced doubt, fear, obstacles, or setbacks in ...

_____
_____
_____
_____
_____

I remember my identity and strength because ...

_____
_____
_____
_____
_____

I saw God move today in ...

_____
_____
_____
_____
_____

## Journaling and Prayer

## Journaling and Prayer

Date: _____

Week 4, Day 6

I found joy, happiness, and fulfillment in ...

_____
_____
_____
_____

I felt concern and response to ...

_____
_____
_____
_____

I felt gratitude for ...

_____
_____
_____
_____

# WEEK 4, DAY 6 | 121

*Then a great and powerful wind tore the mountains apart and shattered the rocks before the LORD, but the LORD was not in the wind. After the wind there was an earthquake, but the LORD was not in the earthquake. After the earthquake came a fire, but the LORD was not in the fire. And after the fire came a gentle whisper.*
***1 Kings 19:11-12 (NIV)***

I experienced doubt, fear, obstacles, or setbacks in ...

_____

_____

_____

_____

_____

I remember my identity and strength because ...

_____

_____

_____

_____

_____

I saw God move today in ...

_____

_____

_____

_____

_____

## Journaling and Prayer

## Journaling and Prayer

Date: _____

Week 4, Day 7

Reoccurring events, emotions, thoughts, words ...

_____
_____
_____
_____

I felt encouraged and strengthened by (people, events, situations) ...

_____
_____
_____
_____

I encouraged others by ...

_____
_____
_____
_____

*Walk in obedience to all that the Lord your God
has commanded you, so that you may live and prosper
and prolong your days in the land that you will possess.*
**Deuteronomy 5:33 (NIV)**

I am sensing a direction toward or away from ...

_____

_____

_____

_____

_____

Next week I will be intentional to ...

_____

_____

_____

_____

_____

Prayer for guidance and direction in ...

_____

_____

_____

_____

_____

## Journaling and Prayer

WEEK 4, DAY 7 | 127

## Journaling and Prayer

# CLOSE
# STEPPING INTO YOUR PURPOSE

*Trust in the LORD with all your heart, And lean not on your own understanding; In all your ways acknowledge Him, and He shall direct your paths.*
*Isaiah 43:19 (NIV)*

God's word is filled with His promises to you. Each promise is true for each individual person who reads it and follows it. Throughout this four-week journal and life study, you have seen that sometimes life's circumstances, situations, and experiences don't make sense to you in the moment. But, through the exercises and reflections, you have begun to see how God's plans and purposes are weaving together in your life and in your daily choices and experiences. The Lord promises that when you choose the truth of His word over your own understanding, He will guide you forward in your path. In all circumstances, pray to the Lord for His wisdom. In your prayers, tell Him when you don't understand; share your fears, concerns, desires, and needs. Tell Him that you are willing to trust Him and that you will choose to follow Him because you trust Him and His word.

## Exercise

For this final exercise, set aside ample time for prayer and reflection. Begin this exercise with prayer and set your heart and mind toward a readiness to seek and hear back from God. You may wish to move through this exercise very slowly, pausing to pray, and using a highlighter or pen to note items of importance and impact. This exercise may take several days depending on how the Lord speaks to you. You may even consider taking time off or traveling to a different location to remove yourself from any distractions. Go to the place that most quiets your mind and the environment that brings you the most peace and closeness to God. You may wish to ask trusted friends and advisors to pray for you in advance of this exercise as you prepare your heart and mind for insight and discovery.

Start your reflection time with this prayer: "Lord, I desire to know your purpose and will for me. Thank you for the past four weeks, and thank you for loving me and caring about me. Thank you for the good plan you have for my life. Thank you for everything you have given me. Thank you for providing for my needs, and thank you for the capabilities you have given to me. Thank you for designing me uniquely, and thank you for the good works that you have prepared for me. Right now, I choose to submit my thoughts to your thoughts, and I ask that the eyes of my spirit see what you want me to see. I am knocking and asking you to open the door to the future you have for me. I commit to you that I will follow the purpose you have for me, and I'm asking you for the strength to do so. I pray that you will never allow me to wander away from you, and I thank you that you will never leave me. When I make a mistake, I will run back to you, and I will receive your forgiveness and restoration to my purpose. Thank you in advance for all that you are going to show me, and thank you in advance for everything you have ahead of me in my life. Amen."

Begin this exercise by reviewing each page of your journal. Read the daily verses at the top of each page and circle anything that stands out to you. Consider each journal entry and assess how each entry and insight resonates with you now. Highlight or underline key phrases or thoughts that impact you, feel like a direction to your spirit, or have insight into your purpose. Consider what thoughts remain the same as when you first wrote them and what thoughts have changed. In a different color pen, cross out what is no longer true, write over the old thoughts with the new thoughts, and add reinforcing thoughts to the entry. As you process and reflect, use the extra journal pages at the end of this book to write down any new thoughts, reactions, questions, or inspirations. If you feel led to stop at any time to pray or to worship, do so. If an action for you to take or the name of a person to connect with comes to mind, write it down. Record reoccurring words, subjects, concepts, and thoughts. If at any time during this exercise you become distracted or unfocused, pause and pray for direction as to whether to continue or to pause and return with a renewed focus. When you have completed your review, write down the overall themes and summarize what you have learned about your purpose.

Now, take all the insights, revelations, and notes you have recorded to create purpose statements and develop a plan of action. You will need help, support, and prayer as you embark on this exciting journey and the following prompts will help you prepare for what is ahead!

The Lord has given me the following talents, skills, gifts, and capabilities:

_____

_____

_____

_____

_____

_____

_____

The Lord has given me a sense of calling and purpose in the following areas:

_____

_____

_____

_____

_____

_____

_____

## CLOSE: STEPPING INTO YOUR PURPOSE

My dream is to:

_____
_____
_____
_____
_____
_____
_____

I will share my dream with, and seek the support of, the following people:

_____
_____
_____
_____
_____
_____

I am taking the following immediate next steps to begin to live out my purpose:

_____
_____
_____
_____
_____
_____

# DESIGNED FOR PURPOSE

I see the following milestones ahead as I pursue my purpose and dreams:

_____
_____
_____
_____
_____
_____

I will commit to the following practices as I continually seek the Lord:

_____
_____
_____
_____
_____
_____

## My Prayer

_____
_____
_____
_____
_____
_____

# YOUR PURPOSE JOURNEY IS JUST BEGINNING

*"I am the vine; you are the branches. If you remain in me and I in you, you will bear much fruit; apart from me you can do nothing."*
*Isaiah 43:19 (NIV)*

Today. This day. You have opened the door to walk a path of purpose toward your destiny, with Jesus leading you and walking with you. This journey is lifelong and eternal. It will include times of excitement and thrill as if a current is sweeping you forward. It will also include times of challenge and testing, and you will feel as though a mountain stands in front of you. Through it all, continue the discipline of putting God's will first through the skills you have developed these past four weeks. Revisit these practices when you encounter uncertainty or when you feel distant from the Lord. Remember the scriptures you have learned and hold them in your heart and mind as you walk in your purpose. Remain in the Lord and watch how He will continue to confirm your purpose and give you the next assignment that He has already prepared for you. Revisit your purpose statements and plans often to stay in alignment with the Lord as He refines you, builds you, and leads you. As you move forward, use the remaining journal pages to record your new experiences and bring your decisions to your heavenly Father in prayer.

## Journaling and Prayer

# Journaling and Prayer

## Journaling and Prayer

## Journaling and Prayer

## Journaling and Prayer

## Journaling and Prayer

## Journaling and Prayer

# Journaling and Prayer

## Journaling and Prayer

## Journaling and Prayer

## Journaling and Prayer

# ABOUT THE AUTHOR

**Tanya Prince** is a purpose coach, leadership consultant, and entrepreneur. After two decades at Fortune 500 companies with a career spanning finance, continuous improvement, and change management. Tanya found her purpose in helping others to thrive and grow personally and professionally.

Tanya is the founder of Green Vine Strategies. As a consultant and coach, she helps leaders and individuals increase their effectiveness through personal excellence, integrity, and authenticity. Tanya has served in womens and youth ministry throughout her entire life, coached young people through high school athletics, and mentored public servants to lead in their communities.

As an author, Tanya combines her love for the truth of God's word with her passion for helping others grow, creating works that help people discover and journey into their purpose and potential. She believes that God has created every person to have a life of meaning and purpose so that they can thrive every single day and have an impact on the world around them. You can learn more about the power of purpose and access encouragement and leadership tools at www.greenvinecoaching.com. Tanya currently resides in Minneapolis, Minnesota, with her children Alexis and Nolan.

# A free ebook edition is available with the purchase of this book.

**To claim your free ebook edition:**

1. Visit MorganJamesBOGO.com
2. Sign your name CLEARLY in the space
3. Complete the form and submit a photo of the entire copyright page
4. You or your friend can download the ebook to your preferred device

### Morgan James BOGO™

A **FREE** ebook edition is available for you or a friend with the purchase of this print book.

CLEARLY SIGN YOUR NAME ABOVE

**Instructions to claim your free ebook edition:**
1. Visit MorganJamesBOGO.com
2. Sign your name CLEARLY in the space above
3. Complete the form and submit a photo of this entire page
4. You or your friend can download the ebook to your preferred device

## Print & Digital Together Forever.

Snap a photo    Free ebook    Read anywhere

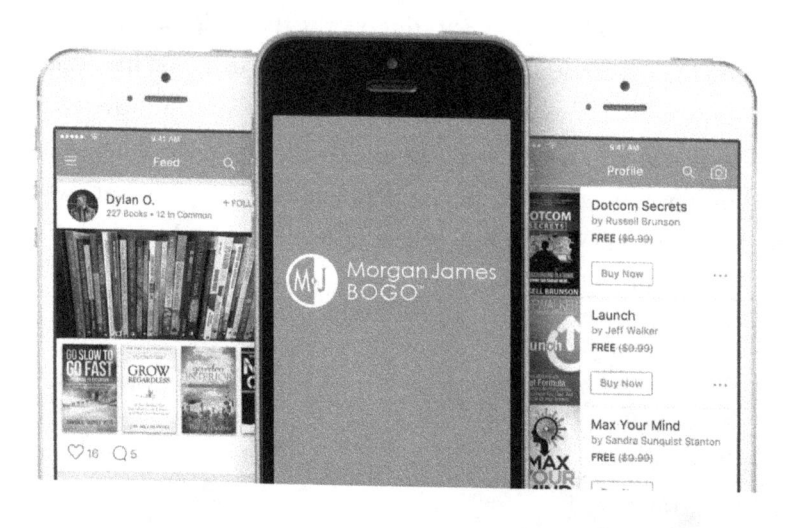